A Bible Christmas

Jesus from A to Z

Written by Catherine Mackenzie   Illustrated by Kezia Hulse

Here is the Christmas story in **ABC**,
the gift of Jesus alphabetically.

Follow the letters and look up the Bible verses.
Use your own Bible or read the verses
at the back of this book.

Aa

The **a**ngels make an **a**nnouncement.
(Luke 2:8-14)

Bb

A **b**aby promised long ago has been **b**orn in **B**ethlehem. (Micah 5:2; Matthew 2:1)

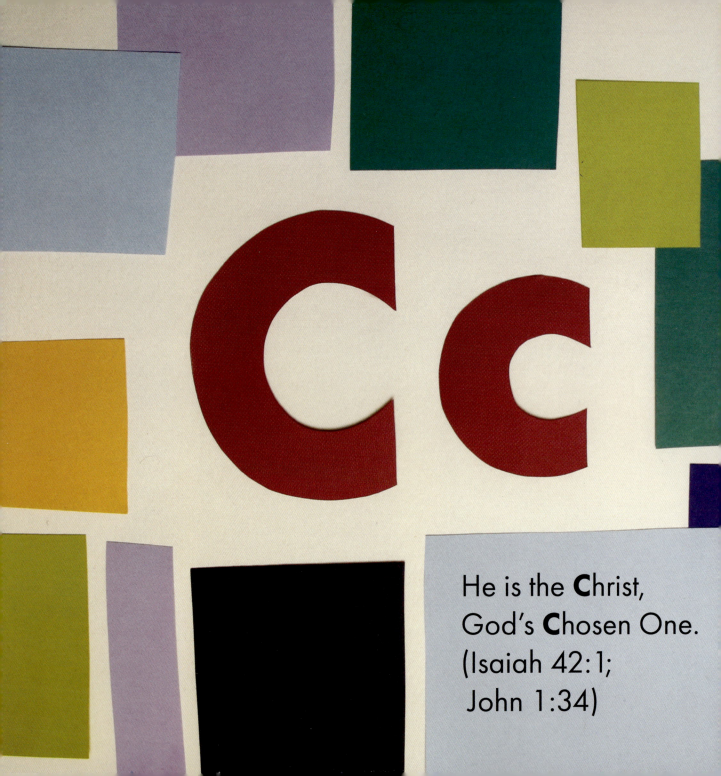

Cc

He is the **C**hrist,
God's **C**hosen One.
(Isaiah 42:1;
John 1:34)

Dd

He is a **d**escendent of King **D**avid. (Luke 1:32)

Ee

He is **e**ternal. His kingdom will never **e**nd. (Luke 1:33)

He is **f**irst and last,

the giver of life. (Revelation 21:6)

He is a **g**ift from **G**od.
(John 3:16)

He is **h**oly. He is perfect and without sin. (John 6:69)

He is called **I**mmanuel which means 'God is with us'. (Isaiah 7:14; Matthew 1:22-23 NLT)

His name is **J**esus. He will save his people from their sins. (Matthew 1:21)

Kk

He is the **l**ight of the world. (John 8:12)

Mm

He is the **M**essiah, the anointed one.
(Matthew 1:16)

Mary and her fiancé Joseph travelled from **N**azareth to Bethlehem.

There was **n**o room for them in the inn. (Luke 2:4-7)

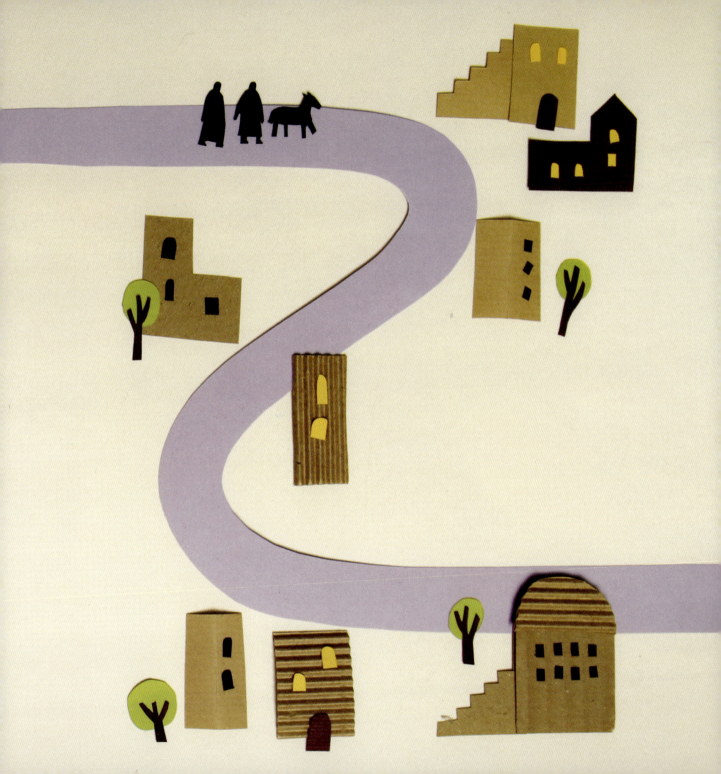

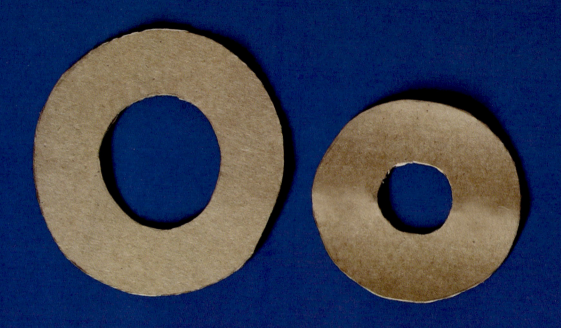

Jesus was born as an **o**rdinary baby. **O**rdinary shepherds visited him in an **o**rdinary stable. Jesus was just like any **o**rdinary human except he never sinned.
(Luke 2:12; Hebrews 4:15)

Pp

Precious gifts of gold, **p**erfume and ointment were **p**resented by the wise men. (Matthew 2:11)

Jesus' mother Mary had **q**uestions. (Luke 1:34)

Rr

Mary would always **r**emember
what she saw and heard. (Luke 2:19)

There were **s**hepherds and a **s**tar. Then Mary heard **S**imeon announce God's **s**alvation. (Luke 2:8; Matthew 2:1-2; Luke 2:30)

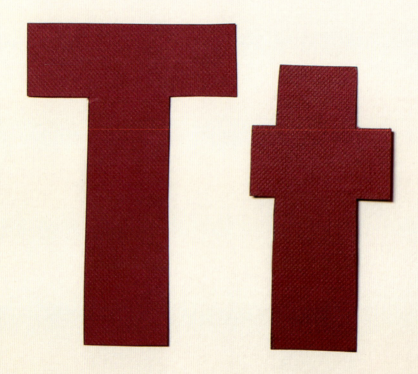

This was in the **t**emple in Jerusalem.
Turtle doves were offered as a sacrifice.
(Luke 2:22-24 ESV)

Uu

He is **v**ictorious. Those who trust in him are **v**ictorious too. (1 Corinthians 15:57)

Jesus came to this **w**orld for one reason .... (1 John 4:14)

... to die on the **X** (cross) to save sinners.

Jesus came back to life and is now in heaven, praying for us. (Romans 8:34)

Yy

He died out of love for sinners like **y**ou and me. (Romans 5:8)

Zz

Jesus is the letter A and the letter **Z** in all things. (Revelation 22:13)

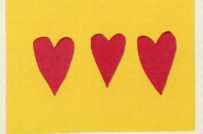

Adore him.
Believe in him.
Come to him.

Luke 2:8-14

And there were shepherds living out in the fields nearby, keeping watch over their flocks at night. An angel of the Lord appeared to them, and the glory of the Lord shone around them, and they were terrified. But the angel said to them, 'Do not be afraid. I bring you good news that will cause great joy for all the people. Today in the town of David a Saviour has been born to you; he is the Messiah, the Lord. This will be a sign to you: you will find a baby wrapped in cloths and lying in a manger.' Suddenly a great company of the heavenly host appeared with the angel, praising God and saying, 'Glory to God in the highest heaven, and on earth peace to those on whom his favour rests.'

Micah 5:2

'But you, Bethlehem Ephrathah, though you are small among the clans of Judah, out of you will come for me one who will be ruler over Israel, whose origins are from of old, from ancient times.'

Matthew 2:1

... Jesus was born in Bethlehem in Judea, during the time of King Herod ...

Isaiah 42:1

'Here is my servant, whom I uphold, my chosen one in whom I delight;
I will put my Spirit on him, and he will bring justice to the nations.'

John 1:34

'I have seen and I testify that this is God's Chosen One.'

Luke 1:32
'He will be great and will be called the Son of the Most High. The Lord God will give him the throne of his father David …'

Luke 1:33
'… and he will reign over Jacob's descendants forever; his kingdom will never end.'

Revelation 21:6
He said to me: 'It is done. I am the Alpha and the Omega, the Beginning and the End. To the thirsty I will give water without cost from the spring of the water of life.'

John 3:16
For God so loved the world that he gave his one and only Son, that whoever believes in him shall not perish but have eternal life.

John 6:69
'We have come to believe and to know that you are the Holy One of God.'

Isaiah 7:14

Therefore the Lord himself will give you a sign: the virgin will conceive and give birth to a son, and will call him Immanuel.

Matthew 1:22-23 (NLT)

All of this occurred to fulfill the Lord's message through his prophet: 'Look! The virgin will conceive a child! She will give birth to a son, and they will call him Immanuel, which means 'God is with us.'

Matthew 1:21

She will give birth to a son, and you are to give him the name Jesus, because he will save his people from their sins.'

Revelation 17:14

They will wage war against the Lamb, but the Lamb will triumph over them because he is Lord of lords and King of kings – and with him will be his called, chosen and faithful followers.'

John 8:12

When Jesus spoke again to the people, he said, 'I am the light of the world. Whoever follows me will never walk in darkness, but will have the light of life.'

Matthew 1:16
'… and Jacob the father of Joseph, the husband of Mary, and Mary was the mother of Jesus who is called the Messiah.'

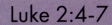
Luke 2:4-7
So Joseph also went up from the town of Nazareth in Galilee to Judea, to Bethlehem the town of David, because he belonged to the house and line of David. He went there to register with Mary, who was pledged to be married to him and was expecting a child. While they were there, the time came for the baby to be born, and she gave birth to her firstborn, a son. She wrapped him in cloths and placed him in a manger, because there was no guest room available for them.

Luke 2:12
'This will be a sign to you: you will find a baby wrapped in cloths and lying in a manger.'

Hebrews 4:15
For we do not have a high priest who is unable to feel sympathy for our weaknesses, but we have one who has been tempted in every way, just as we are – yet he did not sin.

Matthew 2:11
On coming to the house, they saw the child with his mother Mary, and they bowed down and worshipped him. Then they opened their treasures and presented him with gifts of gold, frankincense and myrrh.

Luke 1:34
'How will this be,' Mary asked the angel, 'since I am a virgin?'

Luke 2:19
But Mary treasured up all these things and pondered them in her heart.

Luke 2:8
And there were shepherds living out in the fields nearby, keeping watch over their flocks at night.

Matthew 2:1-2
After Jesus was born in Bethlehem in Judea, during the time of King Herod, Magi from the east came to Jerusalem and asked, 'Where is the one who has been born king of the Jews? We saw his star when it rose and have come to worship him.'

Luke 2:30
'For my eyes have seen your salvation...'

Luke 2:22-24 (ESV)
And when the time came for their purification according to the Law of Moses, they brought him up to Jerusalem to present him to the Lord (as it is written in the Law of the Lord, "Every male who first opens the womb shall be called holy to the Lord") and to offer a sacrifice according to what is said in the Law of the Lord, "a pair of turtle doves, or two young pigeons."

Hebrews 13:8

Jesus Christ is the same yesterday and today and for ever.

1 Corinthians 15:57

But thanks be to God! He gives us the victory through our Lord Jesus Christ.

1 John 4:14

And we have seen and testify that the Father has sent his Son to be the Saviour of the world.

Romans 8:34

Who then is the one who condemns? No one. Christ Jesus who died – more than that, who was raised to life – is at the right hand of God and is also interceding for us.

Romans 5:8

But God demonstrates his own love for us in this: while we were still sinners, Christ died for us.

Revelation 22:13

'I am the Alpha and the Omega, the First and the Last, the Beginning and the End.'

Christian Focus is For Kids

That means you and your friends can all find a book to help you from the CF4KIDS range – from the very littlest baby to kids that are almost too old to be called a kid anymore.

We publish books that introduce you to the real Jesus, the truth of God's Word, and what that means for boys and girls of all ages. Reading books is a fun way to find out what it is like to be a follower of Jesus Christ.
True stories, adventures, activity books, and devotions – they are all here for you and your family.

Christian Focus is part of the family of God.
We aim to glorify Jesus and help you trust and follow Him.

Christian Focus Publications Ltd,
Geanies House, Fearn, Ross-shire, IV20 1TW, Scotland,
United Kingdom.
www.christianfocus.com

Author's Dedication
This book was written because two people introduced me to books from a very early age: William and Carine Mackenzie - thank you!
10 9 8 7 6 5 4 3 2 1
Copyright © 2025 Catherine MacKenzie
ISBN: 978-1-5271-1213-1
Published by Christian Focus Publications,
Geanies House, Fearn, Tain, Ross-shire, IV20 1TW, U.K.
Illustrations by Kezia Hulse
Printed and bound by Imprint, India

All rights reserved. No part of this publication may be reproduced, stored in a retrieval system, or transmitted, in any form, by any means, electronic, mechanical, photocopying, recording or otherwise without the prior permission of the publisher or a licence permitting restricted copying. In the U.K. such licences are issued by the Copyright Licensing Agency, 4 Battlebridge Lane, London, SE1 2HX. www.cla.co.uk